T0065446

# Warrior
## –DESIGNED FOR PURPOSE

30 Day
DEVOTIONAL
FOR WOMAN

# CRISTINA GARCIA

BALBOA.PRESS
A DIVISION OF HAY HOUSE

Balboa Press books may be ordered through booksellers or by contacting:

Balboa Press
A Division of Hay House
1663 Liberty Drive
Bloomington, IN 47403
www.balboapress.com
844-682-1282

Print information available on the last page.

ISBN: 978-1-9822-6067-5 (sc)
ISBN: 978-1-9822-6068-2 (e)

Balboa Press rev. date: 01/27/2021

To my grandmother Milagros Marcial Crespo (July 20, 1926–April 29, 2018). Psalm 4:8 was our favorite verse. She had me memorize the entire chapter in Spanish. I miss you, Abuela. Te amo. Por siempre.

# Contents

# *Acknowledgments*

———⋈———

I want to thank God first for helping me and sustaining me through. I give God all the glory and praise. I don't know where I would be if it had not been for His grace, love, mercy, correction and leading and forgiveness. I thank my spiritual father, Dr. Dennis Bradley Sr., for being the father figure in my life and my therapist for many years. I also thank Dr. Anibal Garcia, another mentor, father figure and former childhood pastor. I thank God for you both.

My beautiful, strong mother brought me up in the ways of the Lord. She is the strongest woman I know. I admire her passion for God and devotion for scripture reading and prayer to the Lord. I admire her love for the Lord and for seeing people come to Christ. I also admire her for being a strong pillar for the family. I love you Mom. Thank you for all you do. I value and appreciate you. You are a blessing from God.

I am thankful for all the people who prayed for me and even people who took their time to encourage me in dark times in my life where I wanted to give up on life in general. I appreciate you. Thank you. Thank you to all those who never gave up on me. Thank you for your encouragement and prayers. I love you. I want to add that because hurt people hurt people and I was extremely hurt for many years in my life. I want to apologize to any person I may have caused hurt or pain due to ignorance, reckless behavior and decisions made by emotions. I pray that God would restore and heal you as well. I take responsibility and own up to things that caused hurt and pain in your life due to my lack of understanding and maturity.

I want to thank Miracle Word Ministries. This ministry has blessed my life tremendously. I thank God for Evangelist Ted Shuttlesworth Jr. and his amazing wife Caroyln ShuttlesWorth. You both are amazing and I love and appreciate you both very much. I also thank God for the Revival Today ministry for Evangelist Johnathan Shuttlesworth and his amazing wife Addalis Shuttlesworth. The entire Shuttlesworth family are all awesome. I'm grateful for these ministries. They bless my life. I thank my awesome church family at Crossroads Community Church in Fitchburg, Massachusetts, including my pastors, Rev. Bryan Tomes and Jessica Tomes. Thank you for your love, prayers, encouragement, and support. A changed life changes lives.

# *Introduction*

*Walking in Victory* a thirty-day devotional book for women's affirmation and declaration. Find healing through the Word of God, making it personal.

Overcome depression, fear, anxiety, low self-esteem, and insecurity. Be confident in who God created you to be. You're valuable to God. Draw close to the heart of Jesus. Confessions and prayers will help draw you closer to the Lord. Make it personal. Find your identity in Christ Jesus. You're more than enough to God. You're not called to be someone else. Be brave, and be the best version of yourself. Find yourself in Jesus. You have a purpose.

Trust God in everything, and believe you are more than enough. Believe what God says about you is true. Don't doubt God's Word. God cannot lie. God created you uniquely with a divine purpose. God can heal your brokenness and restore you to wholeness. You are of great value to God.

Walk daily in forgiveness, acceptance, and soul care. Build yourself up in the Word of God, seeking God's presence and guidance. Be a warrior and not a worrier.

Don't compromise your faith. Stand on the Word of God. Remain in his Word and his Word in You. The world will always leave you empty and unsatisfied, but Christ Jesus will always fill your void. Only in him am I complete and whole. If it costs you your peace, it's too expensive. Guard your heart, mind, peace, and joy. Be selective regarding who you allow into your life.

Prayer is a spiritual force.

Prayer is a conversation with God. It is a mighty weapon against the enemy's schemes. The Word of God intertwined with prayer is a powerful weapon used to stop the enemy in his tracks and cancel his plans of destruction against you and your loved ones. Never allow the busyness of daily tasks or life get in the way of your prayer time with the Lord. As women, we are the pillars of the home and the people God can send to stand in the gap for others in prayer. And when you combine scripture and prayer and make it personal, things begin to shift.

In this thirty-day devotional, my goal is to make it simple but powerful and effective for you to declare the Word of God and help you rewire your mind by using scripture and affirmations will help you gain strength and shine a light of God's truth in sensitive areas where you can gain victory and shut the devil out. And keep him out. The choice is yours to remain a victim to the enemy or take the authority that Christ Jesus has given you already.

We are victorious in Christ Jesus; we fight from a standpoint of victory. Don't let the enemy intimidate you. Take the dominion and power God has given you, use it, and live free daily. The devil is a father of lies, always planting lies in our minds, and too often, we fall victim to his tactics and games. But I say the game is over. We are mighty warriors in the kingdom. We are women of God. We are women of faith, and we are women of courage.

Sometimes we need a fresh reminder of who we are in God. It's our own responsibility to build ourselves up in the Lord. We are not hot messes or prayer projects. My prayer is that after reading this book, you will overcome every lie of the enemy and rewire your mind, feel refreshed, and feel empowered. Speak and believe the Word of God over your life and others. Make it personal, but also pray it over your friends, family, and other loved ones.

I struggled for about a decade and a half. I wasted years of my life stuck on stupid, believing lies of the devil and toxic people. I suffered from verbal abuse that said I wasn't good enough, that I was crazy, and that I wouldn't amount to anything. The ultimate problem is I was a young, immature, naive girl who struggled and always gave up too quickly with low self-esteem issues and was emotionally all over the place—wounded. I was a slave to sin and bound in depression and isolation, battling suicidal thoughts. But I don't need to write an entire story of my failures, mix-ups, and mess-ups to help prove a point.

I learned a lot with all my experiences. They have made me the woman I am today. I am thankful to God for the people he has placed in my life who speak God's truth, and it has helped me tremendously. I rededicated my life to the Lord and have not left the Bible out of sight. The Word of God is the fuel for my soul.

Staying prayerful, praying in tongues, and studying the Word of God will give you supernatural strength and wisdom to make good decisions and have a sensitive awareness of the conviction of the Holy Spirit. He will lead you on the right path. His Word is a lamp unto my feet and keeps me in right standing. The Word of God is my sword for battle. It's what I use to combat the war in my mind. I've learned to use worship, prayer, and fasting along with journaling and reading the scripture to help me win every battle.

I'm alive and survived the battles I went through. I'm able to write this book about what helped me get out of the mess. It's simple really. Sin is the problem. Sin is the root of chaos, pain, sadness, baggage, and destruction in life. Sin is a killer. Sin gives the devil access to destroy your life. If you don't shut the door to sin, it will get rid of you. Sin can destroy your life completely. Once you make the decision to cut off any form of sin from your life—I mean *completely* cut off—you will begin the process of healing and enjoy the life God has always intended for you: a life of peace. Not a problem-free life but a life of victory.

Eliminating sin from your life will give God access into your life. Once you choose Jesus and give your life entirely to Christ and forgive and remove bitterness, anger, rage, and jealousy, you will experience God's abundant life of blessings, provision, joy, peace, wealth, and good health.

This book will be a helpful devotional tool you can add to your personal time with the Lord in prayer. I pray this book blesses, encourages, and opens your eyes to see things the way God sees them—to see yourself the way God sees you. I pray that you may see beneath the exterior. Be inspired.

# Day 1

You are a unique woman. You are a woman of wisdom.

Confession: Say aloud, "I am a woman of wisdom." God will give you wisdom if you ask him for it.

God's wisdom will help you make good choices. God gives generously without finding fault. Ask God for the wisdom you need for today. How can wisdom improve your life? How can it improve your lifestyle?

Scripture: Study and read Proverbs 1:7, James 1:5, and Proverbs 12:15.

Affirmation: I am a woman who depends on the Lord's wisdom and guidance for my everyday life.

# Day 2

You are a woman of purpose. God created you how you are—for special and unique purposes. The world would be a boring place if we looked all the same. Dare to be brave and to be yourself. You don't have to be like someone else. Trying to be something you're not takes away from your unique purpose and authenticity. It's exhausting. Breathe, beautiful. You are amazing.

Confession: Say aloud, "I am a woman with a purpose. It's OK to be myself. There is nothing wrong with me. God makes no mistakes."

Scripture: Read and study Proverbs 16:3 and Psalm 139:14 (AMP). Affirmation: I am thankful that God made me unique and with a purpose.

# *Day 3*

I am a woman who is able to forgive. Jesus had every right if he wanted to curse people out, not choose to die for us on the cross and be done, but Jesus showed us compassion, love, and forgiveness. He better than anyone knows pain, suffering, trauma, betrayal, and hurt, yet he showed us the pathway of forgiveness. Now you may have been done dirty—maybe betrayal, abuse, relationship issues, church hurt, family drama, or whatever the case may be—but God can help you walk in love and forgiveness. You don't have to reconnect with toxic people who hurt you, but you can choose the path of forgiveness and always wish and pray for their well-being. Set healthy boundaries. However, there is someone you can never run away from or block, and that is yourself.

In order to forgive others, you must first forgive yourself. Self-forgiveness continues to be my pathway to self-love. Self-forgiveness makes space for new beginnings in my life. Self-forgiveness offers me permission to let go a little more. Self-forgiveness creates compassion in my heart and openness to forgive others. Don't be a doormat, but yes, forgiveness is the greatest gift you can give yourself. Pause a moment, pray, and ask God to search your heart. Ask him to help you let go completely. God knows it hurts; however, forgiveness is humbling and helps you draw closer to the heart of God. There is healing in forgiveness.

I'm sorry this is longer than the other ones, but this is very important. Unforgiveness is a sin that leads to bitterness, rage, anger, and jealousy. Unforgiveness contaminates your soul and can make you sick. Find healing in genuine forgiveness through the power of God's love and Word.

Confession: I am a woman who is able to forgive. Scripture: Read and meditate on Matthew 6:14.

Affirmation: I am able to forgive myself and others and receive God's

forgiveness in my life.

Prayer: Lord, may we choose forgiveness and love for ourselves and others always. Amen.

God will help you. Forgiveness isn't a feeling. Forgiveness is a choice. Set yourselffree.

# Day 4

You are a brave and strong woman.

Confession: Say aloud, "I am not afraid; I am strong, brave, and beautiful." Scripture: Read Joshua 1:9, 2 Timothy 1:7, and Philippians 4:13.

Affirmation: If God commands it, I must do it. I am more than capable. I am strong. My strength is in Christ Jesus.

# Day 5

I am a woman of joy.

Confession: Say aloud, "I will choose to not be led by my emotions today. I choose joy."

Train your mind to see things in a different perspective. Life sometimes can be challenging; however, God has already given you the victory. Don't live a life of defeat when Christ Jesus has already given you the victory. Choose the joy of the Lord. It makes the devil happy to see you down in the dumps. Don't give him the satisfaction. Just because you have made mistakes in the past or have failed, it does not make you a mistake or a failure. God has given you the victory to enjoy life today and the wisdom to create a bright future. Get excited. God has a plan for your life. Get up, pretty lady. Choose the joy of the Lord.

Scripture: Proverbs 31:25.

# Day 6

You are enough! You are *you,* and that is your power!

Don't fall into the trap of comparison. Comparison stripes you away from all joy. Don't let the devil make you play that game. Save your energy and compete with who you were yesterday. Strive to become a better version of yourself. Be hungry to grow, and don't let anything stop you, but always be humble. We all poop, and it smells. But we can all shine as brightly as we want. Go ahead and sparkle. Strive for excellence, and do your best at being yourself. Nobody can do you best like you can. Now it's totally OK to get inspired by another woman, but don't kill yourself trying to be like her. If the shoe fits, wear it, but if it doesn't fit, give it away. Flowers in gardens never ask permission to bloom; they just do. Bloom, shine, and grow. You are enough. "Pride is your greatest enemy; humility is your greatest friend," said the late John R. W. Stott. Make no mistake about it: pride is the greatest sin. It is the devil's most effective and destructive tool. Make sure you copy the right cat.

Confession: I am enough.

Scripture: James 4:7–8; James 4:10; Acts 17:28.

Affirmation: I will let God lift me up. I am nothing without God.

# Day 7

I am a woman of vision.

Scripture: Read Psalm 32:8 and Psalm 139:14 (AMP).

What is blocking your sight? How do you see yourself? (Journal.)

Affirmation: I am what God says that I am. I refuse the spirit of doubt. Tell me otherwise. God tells no lies.

# Day 8

I am a woman of influence.

In the Bible are many women who were influencers. What can you learn from them to inspire you to influence the world around you in a positive way?

Hannah, Esther, Abigail, Elizabeth, Anna, Miriam, Sarah, Rebekah, Deborah, Ruth, Mary, and many more. I challenge you to read about them and write down things you can learn from them. Find things that will inspire you, and apply them to your life.

Confession: I am a woman of value and of great importance. I am a godly woman.

# Day 9

You are a woman of character.

How can being a woman of character improve my everyday life? How can I become better?

Scripture: Study and read Romans 5–4 and the book of Proverbs. Get some girls together and have a Bible study party. Grab some coffee, tea, or a healthy, yummy smoothie. And grow together.

# Day 10

You are a woman of discipline.

Scripture: 2 Timothy 1:7; Ephesians 6:4; Proverbs 12:1; Proverbs 10:17. You can do it.

How can you develop a life of discipline? Confession: I am a woman of discipline.

Affirmation: I will do what I need to do with the help of God.

# Day 11

You are a powerful woman.

Scripture: Romans 10:8; Mark 16:17–18.

Speak with authority when the attack comes. Command the devil to leave in the name of Jesus Christ. Confession: I am powerful.

You are created in the image of God. Don't let the devil intimidate you. He is the one who is intimidated. He sees God in you.

Affirmation: I am a powerful woman in the Lord. God's power is more than enough.

# Day 12

You are a woman and a warrior.

Prayer is essential. Faith is a fight. Faith without works is dead. Walk out your faith boldly and fearlessly. Prayer is about establishing a relationship with God and building your faith and trust in him. He can be trusted.

Confession: Prayer is my superpower.

Scripture: James 5:16; Psalm 4:1; Psalm 32:6; Psalm 39:12.

Affirmation: I will always win the victory because of my dedication of time spent with the Lord in prayer.

# Day 13

You are a beautiful woman. Confession: I am beautiful.

Scripture: Proverbs 21:3; 1 John 2:29; 2 Timothy 2:22. What makes you beautiful?

Affirmation: I am the righteousness of God.

# Day 14

You are a woman after God's own heart. Confession: I am a woman after God's own heart. How will you grow closer to the heart of God?

Scripture: Matthew 6:33.

Affirmation: I don't seek the blessings. I seek the heart of God.

# Day 15

You are a godly woman

Confession: I am a woman who walks in holiness .

Fasting is a tool to use along with prayer. It sets you apart for special goldy assignments, breaks chains, and causes healing and massive breakthroughs both for yourself and others. It helps you draw closer to God and helps keep your flesh under control.

Scripture: Joel 2:12; Nehemiah 1:4; Ezra 8:23; Esther 4:16; Daniel 9:3. How will you add a lifestyle of fasting and prayer to help you grow spiritually?

Affirmation: Fasting along with prayer will give me access to operate in the supernatural.

# Day 16

You're a woman who radiates light and is walking in overflowing joy. Confession: I am always overflowing with joy.

Scripture: "You love righteousness and hate wickedness; therefore God, Your God has anointed you with the oil of gladness more than your companions" (Psalm 45:7).

Affirmation: I am anointed with the oil of gladness. I will rejoice.

# Day 17

You are a woman free from burdens

Confessions: I am not meant to carry burdens; I'm meant to carry blessings. Scripture: First Peter 5:7 says, "Cast your cares on the Lord." Affirmation: God cares for me!

# Day 18

You're a woman of purpose.

Confession: I have purpose. God has a plan for my life. It's a good plan. Scripture: Jeremiah 29:11.

Affirmation: I have a future filled with good things. I have hope. I have a purpose.

# Day 19

You are a woman who values wisdom.

Confession: I am a woman who values the wisdom of the Lord. Scripture: Proverbs 3:2–9.

Affirmation: I will honor the Lord with my wealth. Everything I touch is blessed.

# Day 20

Women of God are helped by the Lord. Confession: The Lord God sustains me. Scripture: Isaiah 41:10.

Affirmation: God sustains me with his righteous right hand.

# Day 21

You are a woman who will do exploits for the kingdom of God. Confession: I am a woman who will do exploits for the kingdom of God. Scripture: Daniel 11:32 People that know God, Because I know God.

Affirmation: I will do exploits in the strength of my God.

# Day 22

You are a virtuous woman. Confession: I am a woman of virtue. Scripture: Study and read Proverbs 31.

# Day 23

You are a woman who is Holy Spirit led.

Confession: It's the consistency of my actions that will bring ultimate change. I don't ask my body how it's doing; I tell it how it's doing. (Subdue your flesh on a daily basis.)

Scripture: 1 Corinthians 9:27. John 16:13

Affirmation: My flesh is an enemy of my personal revival. I will not be led by my flesh. The spirit of God will guide me into all truth.

# *Day 24*

You're not a woman led by emotion.

Confession: I am a woman of self-control. The Holy Spirit is my helper. Scripture: Galatians 5:22–23.

Affirmation: I have soul control!

# Day 25

Women of God don't walk alone. We lack no good things. Confession: I don't walk alone. God walks with me daily. Scripture: Isaiah 49:16; James 4:8; Philippians 4:19. John 16:13 Affirmation: God has my back.

# Day 26

You are a confident woman.

Confession: I am a woman of God, and I am secure in Christ Jesus. I am secure in my Lord and Savior.

Scripture: 1 Samuel 16:7; Psalm 139:14; 1 Corinthians 10:13. Psalm 16:8 Affirmation: I am confident in God.

# Day 27

Women of God are favored by the Lord.

Confession: I am a woman of God and favored by the Lord. The favor of the Lord is my shield.

Scripture: Psalm 5:11–12.

Affirmation: I am surrounded by the favor of the Lord as a shield.

# Day 28

You are a woman of faith.

Confession: I please the Lord because of my faith. Scripture: Hebrews 11:6; Matthew 21:21; Mark 11:23. Affirmation: My faith moves mountains.

# Day 29

You are anointed. We respect each other. Confession: I am anointed to do all things.

Scripture: 1 John 2:27; 1 John 2:20; Isaiah 10:27; Psalm 105:15. Affirmation: I am a carrier of the presence of God.

# Day 30

You are a woman of integrity, dignity, and great value. Confession: I am a woman of dignity and modesty. I am of great value. Scripture: Proverbs 31:25.

Affirmation: If I have God, I have it all.

Insecurity is the root of being exposed, and in being exposed, we fear the exposure of our imperfections and weaknesses. The solution is to rest in our perfect God. God covers us. I can rest in a perfect, all-knowing God. It's OK that I don't have all the answers, and it's OK that I'm not perfect. I'm growing and learning. God covers our sins, our weaknesses, and our vulnerability. Just because I feel insecure doesn't mean I have to be insecure. For example, I don't have to get in an argument with someone and belittle them to feel good about myself because I feel insecure. Nor do I have to get into an argument and defend myself. God defends me. Choose your battles wisely. Save your energy.

Confession: God is my defense; he is my defender. (Read Psalm 27:3–5 and Psalm 27:10.)

We are hidden in Christ Jesus. Our identity doesn't have to be based on what others think or say. When we are accepted by God (Psalm

27:10), there is no room for insecurity in the heart of a woman who stands in the Word of truth: the living, effective, powerful Word of almighty God.

We are fully accepted, loved, and defended by God. Women of God don't need to walk in fear, insecurity, or low self-esteem. When we stand on the Word of God, we are his beloved.

# About the Author

My name is Cristina Iris Garcia. I was born and raised in Leominster Massachusetts. I am a Christian speaker, singer, songwriter, author, makeup artist, skin-care specialist, and senior independent beauty consultant with Mary Kay Cosmetics. My dream is to be a blessing and encourage as many women in a powerful positive way to help build confidence and to share the gospel of Jesus Christ to as many people as possible. God set me free from depression, suicidal thoughts, and an eating disorder. God healed me from toxic relationships, abuse, and low self-esteem. God opened my eyes and brought healing and peace to my life. My prayer is that this book will bless the hearts of many who read it. If you find yourself in a dark place I encourage you to seek out for help if needed. I pray God would heal, restore and bless you just like He has done for me.

# The Prayer of Salvation

Heavenly Father, thank you for sending your Son, Christ Jesus, to die for me. I believe that you raised him from the dead and that he is coming back soon.

I'm asking you to forgive me of my sins and to make me brand new. Give me holy desires to pray and read your Word. Empower me by your Holy Spirit to live for you the rest of my life.

You are the Lord of my life. I thank you that the old life is gone and a new life has begun.

In Jesus's name, amen.

Printed in the United States
By Bookmasters

This book is a book of affirmations and devotion to help Christian women be build up in their confidence using Bible verses and a opportunity to journal down and grow in a relationship with God.

I am a fun optimistic, energetic,strong Smart ,funny charismatic Christian woman.  Discovering new and beautiful things about who I am everyday. I'm a singer,songwriter,author and life couch and public speaker. Born and raised in twin city Massachusetts. I love to make people feel good about themselves and bring encouragement and joy to those around me. My mission is to use every gift and talent God gave me to bless everyone I encounter. Life is gift and I realized after battling chronic depression,suicidal thoughts, ptsd and healing from toxic relationships,I realized I have value and have so much to offer to the people around me. It's my choice to keep going and not let gloomy days keep me down. God is my source of strength and my mother is my motivation. I'm grateful to God for the people I have in my life that never gave up on me. For that I am forever grateful. Life can be challenging. I think God created each one of us with a unique purpose and destiny. It's up to you to embrace it and dig deep within yourself to bring become your best self in God and bring hope, joy and love to the people around you. We all have something wonderful to discover and bring to the table. I pray God will help you dig deep with in yourself and be everything he created you to be. We just have to search a little deeper and you will find your true self. My hope is that some how I can make a difference in the life's of many. Girls compete, woman empower. Let's empower, and be great!

U.S. $8.99

ISBN 978-1-9822-6067-
5089

**BALBOA**.PRESS
A DIVISION OF HAY HOUSE

9 781982 260675

**Malthouse**

# Our Wife
# HAS GONE MAD

## (a play)

**'Bode Ojoniyi**